Gifts of the Holy Spirit

By Kathryn Kuhlman

Gifts of the Holy Spirit

Resolution on the Holy Spirit

The Holy Spirit is the spirit of God. He inspired holy men of old to write the scriptures. Through illumination He enables men to understand truth. He exalts Christ. He convicts of sin, of righteousness and of judgement. He calls men to the saviour, and effects regeneration. He cultivates Christian character, comforts believers, and bestows the spiritual gifts by which they serve God through His Church. He seals the believer unto the day of final redemption. His presence in the Christian is the assurance of God to bring the believer into the fullness of the stature of Christ. He enlightens and empowers the believer and the church in worship, evangelism, and service.

"Now concerning spiritual gifts, brethren, i would not have you ignorant. Ye know that ye were Gentiles, carried away unto these dumb idols, even as ye were led. Wherefore I give you to understand, that no man speaking by the spirit of God calleth Jesus accursed: and that no man can say that Jesus is the Lord, but by the Holy Ghost.

" Now there are diversities of gifts, but the same Spirit. And there are differences of administrations, but the same Lord. And there are diversities of operations, but it is the same God which worketh all in all. But the manifestation of the Spirit is given to every man to profit withal.

" For to one is given by the Spirit the word of wisdom; to another the word of knowledge by the same Spirit; to another faith by the same Spirit; to another the gifts of healing by the same Spirit; to another the working of miracles; to another prophecy; to another discerning of spirits; to another divers kind of tongues; to another the interpretation of tongues: but all these worketh that one and the selfsame Spirit, dividing to every man severally as he will."(1 Corinthians 12:1-11)

CHAPTER 1

The Purpose of God's Gifts

Together, we are going to have one of the most interesting and informative studies that we have ever had. I want you to enter into this series on the Gifts of the Holy Spirit, with your Bible open and with an open mind, as the Holy Spirit Himself becomes our teacher. It is He who holds the key to a successful, fruitful, and victorious Christian life and through His gifts, we glorify God's Son, Jesus Christ. There are two extremes which we face today as we come to the subject of spiritual gifts. First of all, there is abuse. Some have brought a reproach upon the wonderful work of the Holy Spirit because of their misappropriation of the supernatural power of the Spirit. I think most of us could cite examples of fanaticism arising around this doctrine; and because this doctrine has suffered much abuse, there is the second extreme: the average child of God has neglected it and does not know the teaching of the word of God in the matter of spiritual gifts. Lest he be deemed a fanatic or thought to run to the same excesses to which many have gone, the average Christian shies away from the teaching of the word of God in his quest for spiritual gifts.

I want you to see something. The gifts of the Holy Spirit are capacities for service. They are given for service and service alone. Paul named some of the gifts in the 12th Chapter of 1 Corinthians, and I want to inject something here that is most important. We always speak of the NINE gifts of the Spirit. We accept the fact that the gifts number nine, and that exhausts the supply.

Why do we take so much for granted? Why are we so quick to limit God? Don't limit God to just nine gifts when His supply is exhaust less. Paul has named nine gifts in writing to the Corinthians, but there are more. The gifts of the Holy Spirit are given " to every man severally as the Holy Spirit wills." We are individuals in His sight and God knows us better than we know ourselves, and gives us gifts that are suited to each one of His children. We consider the day in which we live so modern and up-to-date, but the Apostle Paul dealt with problems not unlike many which the churches are facing today; ignorance concerning spiritual gifts. This ignorance on the part of the average professing Christian involves not only spiritual gifts, but ignorance concerning the Holy Spirit Himself. We need some good, sound Biblical teaching regarding this Third Person of the Trinity.

Therefore, let us study carefully this person and this subject which is of vital importance to the ministry of the Word of God that we may discover the part that each individual has in the ministry.

Remember, there is just one Holy Spirit! He is the same Third Person of the Trinity who fills the vessel and baptizes with the Spirit, that gives gifts aside from these wonderful gifts of Himself. Much abuse has been brought upon the things of the Spirit, in exactly the same way that much disorder and confusion were evidenced in the lives of the assembly of the Corinthians church. This was, and is now, because of the basic misunderstanding of the Person of the Holy Spirit and His gifts.

CHAPTER 2

My Glory Will I Not Give to Another (Isaiah 42:8)

If you are a little cautious, if you are a little loath to accept some things labelled 'the work of the Holy Spirit', one of the greatest criterions that I can give you is this: the Holy Spirit will always glorify, will always edify, will always promote Jesus and Jesus only!

So many times, I have wished that I could have been at that great Conference Table when the Father, Son, and the Holy Spirit laid the plan for mankind's salvation, to hear from Jesus' lips His offer to come and take upon Himself the form of man. Each member of the Trinity had a definite part in our salvation, and I can almost hear the Holy Spirit say: " I will be there to take over the work of glorifying Jesus on the earth and in the hearts of men and women." The Holy Spirit is the greatest promoter who ever lived, and He Promotes just one person: Jesus Christ, the son of the living God. If you never remember another word I say, if you never read another of my messages, remember this as long as you live: when it is the Holy Spirit manifesting His power, He will always edify and glorify JESUS, not some personality.

We have all seen men and women in religious work who do everything in the world to bring glory to themselves and to their own name. The Holy Spirit does not glorify an individual. Never! It is Jesus whom He glorifies, and it was Jesus Himself who said, "if I will be lifted from the earth, I will draw all men unto me." (John 12:32).

Paul, the mighty spiritual giant, understood perfectly, and one of the most profound things he ever said is found in 1 Timothy 1:15: "Christ Jesus came into the world to save sinners; of whom I am CHIEF." In spite of Paul's great spiritual revelations and his mountaintop experiences; in spite of his glorious knowledge of the things of God, he counted himself to be the least, the chief of sinners. He acknowledged himself as nothing and never tried to build an

empire for himself or promote himself.

This explains why the Holy Spirit, through that yielded vessel, lifted up Jesus; and as Jesus was lifted up, lives were gloriously transformed by the power of God. There lies the secret to Paul's ministry and to our personal witness for the Lord Jesus Christ today.

CHAPTER 3

'Thus Saith the Lord'

Nothing is as powerful as the written word of God. If I say one thing and the Bible teaches another, the Bible is right. If your church or pastor teaches one thing and the Bible says another, the Bible is right. Sometimes I think it's the hardest thing in the world for folk to turn away from their preconceived ideas and come back again to the word of God. It will be a wonderful day when all professing Christians, regardless of denomination, get back to the Word of God, back again to "thus saith the Lord." We have so much 'churchology, ' so much theory, so much creed. There is too much of man's doctrine and too little of " thus saith the Lord."

Let me repeat a statement I made before: there is only ONE Holy Spirit, and if you think I am stressing this fact too strongly, perhaps the experience I cite here will help you to understand: I stood before a great congregation with the Holy Spirit using this vessel, speaking through lips of clay, very conscious of the anointing of the Holy Ghost upon my body. The Holy Spirit was molding hearts, in readiness to receive Christ; then, suddenly, there was an interruption by someone in the audience, a distraction as that one began speaking in tongues or giving a personal testimony.

Hear me! There is but ONE Holy Spirit. He does not interrupt Himself as He speaks through a vessel bringing a message of eternal life. After that one has finished speaking, it is a different matter entirely for "there are diversities of gifts," and we are all members of one Body; but let us remember that all things must be "done decently and in order." (1 Corinthians 14:40) God is not a God of confusion or disorder, but of peace and harmony, instructing and edifying and encouraging His people.

CHAPTER 4

The Holy Spirit: Person or Gift?

Let me make something very clear as we lay the foundation of our study of the individual gifts of the Holy Spirit. There is a difference between receiving one or more of the spiritual gifts, and that glorious experience of being filled with the spirit. When it comes to that wonderful experience of being filled with the Spirit (perhaps you refer to it as the Baptism of the Holy Spirit), always remember that it is a definite, spiritual experience separate and apart from being born again; and if you are a member of the body of Christ, if you have been born into God's family, born into His church, this experience is for you. It doesn't matter what your religious affiliation may be or where you have your church membership. If you have been born into the body of Christ, then this wonderful experience of being filled with the Spirit is a part of your inheritance.

Turn to the Second Chapter of the Book of Acts. There we read about this glorious experience in the Upper Room when the Holy Spirit came, and they were all filled with the Spirit. Then peter, speaking under the anointing of the Holy Spirit to the Jews and devout men gathered in Jerusalem, said: " Repent, and be baptized every one of you in the name of Jesus Christ for the remission of sins, and ye shall receive the gift of the Holy Ghost. For the promise is unto you and to your children and, to ALL that are afar off, even as many as the Lord our God shall call." (Acts 2:38, 39)

I believe that the Holy Spirit, speaking through the lips of Peter, was very careful to make it clear lest someone should say this experience of being filled with the Spirit was for the Early Church only. The Holy Spirit made it all- inclusive, for "the promise is unto you, and to your children, and to all that are afar off, even as many as the Lord our God shall call." If you have been called to be a Christian, called to be an heir of God and a joint-heir with Christ Jesus, then you have been called to be filled with the Spirit. This is a part of your inheritance.

Many of you are going around emaciated and half-starved spiritually. It's no wonder you cannot influence anyone else. It's no wonder folk look at you and think, "if that is what it means to be a Christian, I don't want it because there is no joy and there is no power and there's no life!" When you possess everything that

Jesus has made possible to you as a Christian, you will enjoy your inheritance, and you will be the happiest person in the world. So, go out and start possessing your possessions now!

Now, don't misunderstand and think I am implying that there won't be sorrows and disappointments in your Christian walk. I'm not saying that you'll never be sick physically, for not one of us is immune to sickness or disease. Not one of us is immune to sorrow or to heartbreak and disappointment. In fact, Jesus said that we would not only have troubles, but we would have tribulation! Yet, in spite of these things, we can be victorious; we can have a confidence inside of us that is unshakable. God has provided a power through the person of the Holy Spirit that will cause us to rise above our troubles. They will not defeat us, and we will not only be conquerors over the misfortunes that happen in our lives, but we will be MORE than conquerors through the Christ who loves us. We will possess an inner joy; we will possess a confidence knowing that nothing can happen to us but that which God allows and permits. We can rest in the assurance that whatever comes into our lives, we can USE that thing for spiritual growth and progress, and for God's glory.

An unsaved person and a child of God may encounter the same problem, they may be confronted with the very same situation, which will defeat the unsaved man or woman. Yet, a similar circumstance in the life of a Christian will be used for the glory of God, and to bring spiritual growth that will strengthen that one's character. That's the kind of salvation, the kind of spirituality, that I believe in. It's a daily proposition, a day-by-day walk, and it works!

CHAPTER 5

14

A Gift Is a Gift

How can I explain to you the real meaning of a gift? Some folk live and die without ever knowing what it means to really give a gift - without 'strings' attached or without a purpose behind the gift. When the Holy Spirit gives, it is real giving and genuine love prompts the gifts that He gives. Until we have experienced God's giving to us, we really do not know HOW to give or understand all that is involved in giving.

Only God knows how much I want the best that He has for me and I sincerely covet the best of His gifts. I can covet a gift, but nowhere in the Word of God does it say that we are to beg for His gifts. His giving is spontaneous, something that He does out of His great heart. I try to live pleasing to Him, wanting so much to be in the position where... How can I say it? I can't use the word 'worthy' for His gifts are not merited, they are not given because we are worthy, for not one of us is worthy of God's blessing. In other words, we cannot 'work' for a gift. Gifts are given because the giver wants to give, and his gifts come from the heart.

Let me give you an example. You work for your paycheck. You put long hours into a day's work. You earn and receive your salary, but a gift is something different. It is given to you, although you never worked for it - it isn't a reward for something you have done - it is not given because you begged for the gift. It is given because the giver wanted to give the gift, and in giving, he receives a joy as great as you to whom the gift was given.

In exactly the same way that the Holy Spirit controls the giving of His gifts, He will also control each gift itself. Turn to 1 Corinthians 12:7; "The manifestation of the Spirit is given to every man to profit withal." We see here that the gifts of the Spirit are called "manifestation of the Spirit." Wherever we see "gifts of the Spirit" in operation - whether it is the gift of healing, or the gift of faith, or the gift of Miracles, or the gift of wisdom or of knowledge, always know that it is the "Manifestation of the Spirit." Therefore, if one has been given a gift of the Spirit and that one knows that he has been given a gift, he will not speak of it and will not boast of it, for he will recognize the fact that it is nothing of himself - it is the Manifestation of the Spirit.

The Spirit does these wonderful things through a body. It is not some natural ability that the Holy Spirit blesses. All that the individual furnishes is the body, the vessel, the willingness, the complete surrender to God of body and soul and spirit. Jesus, Himself, had to surrender wholly to the father and to the Holy Spirit before He could be used in His Earthly ministry. Even to those last hours in the Garden of Gethsemane when He faced the cross, Jesus, with a will separate and apart from the will of the father, had to yield His own will to the father's will: "Nevertheless not as I will, but as thou wilt." (Mathew 26: 39). When we yield ourselves completely to God, He will take that vessel and use it, but it is HIS POWER. It is the Holy Spirit Himself who gives the manifestation.

God knows that never once in my life have I professed to have a gift. I feel that whatever the Holy Spirit has entrusted to me is something so sacred, so precious, a treasure that is the Manifestation of the Spirit and nothing of Kathryn Kuhman. Not a saint who ever possessed anything of himself where of he could boast. Paul, one of the greatest religious leaders of all time, never uttered a boastful word regarding the gifts of the Spirit that were manifested through his life. Why? Because the deeper one goes in his concentration, the more he realizes that he is absolutely nothing without the power of God. Without the manifestation of the Holy Ghost, man is just flesh and blood and bone. It is the Spirit, The Holy Ghost, who gives the power.

That is the reason why the gifts of the Spirit are called "manifestations of the Spirit." The apostles could do the supernatural things only as they were moved upon by the Spirit. When we read the account of the apostles regarding the manifestations of the power of God in their lives, we marvel, and we thrill. But remember something! It is the same Holy Spirit that you and I know and these precious apostles, the Christians in the early church, could do the supernatural things only as they were moved upon by the spirit. Jesus Himself could do those great and mighty works only as He was moved upon by the Spirit.

We have all read that glorious incident in acts 3:1-11 when peter and John came upon the lame man at the gate called Beautiful. Peter, no doubt, had seen that lame man scores of times, for day after day he was among the beggars at the temple gate; and the apostles, having established a church in Jerusalem, met daily in the temple long before this lame man was healed. But it wasn't until Peter was moved upon by the Spirit, that he spoke to him. In that moment, the Holy Spirit came upon Peter, and he was given, by the Spirit, that wonderful gift of healing. Had he tried to heal the lame man without the Spirit, nothing would have happened; for without the Holy Spirit and without the gift of the Spirit, and without the power of the Spirit, peter was an ordinary Christian, saved by the grace of God. It is nothing of ourselves, "It is God that worketh in you both to will and to do of his good pleasure." (Philippians 2:13).

We all know there are men and women who are NATURALLY gifted or talented, who by birth have higher intelligence and greater abilities which place them head and shoulders above others. In your own family - perhaps among your children - one is more intelligent than another. That one was born to the same parents, grew up in the same home, under the same environment, and had the same advantages. Yet it is easy for that one to learn and make the highest grade in school - easier than for a brother or sister who earns just average grades, but works harder than the other child. Understand it? You can't.

On the other hand, when we speak of the gifts of the Spirit, we are not talking about folk who are naturally more intelligent. We are speaking of a supernatural endowment. They may not be especially gifted 'in the natural,' but when it comes to spiritual things, they know more about the word of God, understanding the Bible better, than somebody who has earned many degrees or has gone to a theological seminary. What is the difference? It is the same thing that Paul is speaking about in the twelfth Chapter of 1 Corinthians: a supernatural endowment of the Holy Spirit.

Please turn to 1 Corinthians, chapter 12, the First Verse, and read what Paul said: "Now concerning spiritual gifts, brethren, I would not have you ignorant." We know by the word 'brethren' that Paul is not talking to the unregenerated. He is not talking to those who know nothing about spiritual things. He is speaking to those who are members of the Body of Christ and is dealing with a subject about which they were ignorant. Paul wanted to let them know that the gifts he was talking about could be theirs.

If you are a healthy Christian and there is spiritual growth in your life - if you are living daily as a victorious Christian, then there will be a desire in your heart for more of Jesus and more of the things of the Spirit. Do not feel there is something wrong with you if you are dissatisfied, and if you find deep within yourself a sincere hunger and desire for more of God, for more of the knowledge of His Word. That's the surest sign that you are a healthy Christian. You should be greatly alarmed and disturbed if you do not hunger for the things of the Spirit, if you do not desire a deeper experience with God, if you have come to the place where you are satisfied. The word of God says, "Blessed are they which do hunger and thirst after righteousness: for they shall be filled."(Mathew 5: 6)

I have never walked away from a miracle service after having seen the glorious manifestation of God's power, but that I feel an intense hunger for greater things than I have seen. Why? Because I know that somehow, someplace, I have limited God and there are resources in Christ Jesus that I have not yet tapped. The greatest saint who ever lived never received ALL that God had for that individual. Therefore, do not be afraid of the things of the Spirit. Covet, and covet earnestly, all that the Holy Spirit has for you, and you can always be sure that He gives the gift that is best suited to you. He will not give you a gift that does not complement your personality or fails to take into consideration your desires and your weaknesses. Our lord is always a wise giver.

CHAPTER 6

The Lordship of Christ

The religious background of the Christians in Corinthians differed greatly from Paul's training in the Jew's religion. In their unconverted days, they knew nothing about the living God, the law of Moses, of the miracles performed through the Old Testament prophets. "Ye know that ye were Gentiles, carried away unto these dumb idols, even as ye were led." (1 Corinthians 12:2). Here, Paul uses the words 'carried away' suggesting satanic power; and there is satanic power behind all idolatry. "Wherefore I give you to understand, that no man speaking by the Spirit of God calleth Jesus accursed: and that no man can say that Jesus is the Lord, but by the Holy Ghost."(verse 3).

We readily see that the apostles mark the clear-cut dividing line between Christianity and every system of man's devices. There is something more than sincerity, for one can be sincerely wrong, one can be a very religious person, extremely religious, in fact, and very sincere in keeping his religion; and yet, in the final analysis, he can be sincerely wrong in his sincerity. Any religion that denies the deity and divinity of Jesus Christ, any religion that denies the atoning blood of the son of the Living God, is not Christian but anti-Christian. It makes all the difference in the world what you do with Jesus Christ, the son of the Living God.

Christianity, and Christianity alone, exalts Jesus Christ as the very Son of God, accepts His deity and divinity. Other systems deny His lordship and think of Him as accursed, for it is only by the Holy Spirit that we recognize Jesus' lordship.

Have you ever gone through Paul's epistle to the Corinthians and counted the number of times he used the title 'lord' as applied to our wonderful Saviour? This is truly the epistle of the lordship of Christ, and we are called upon to always recognize His lordship, His absolute authority over our hearts and our lives. Under all circumstances, remember that the Holy Spirit recognizes the lordship of Jesus; and you and I, as members of His body, must also recognize His absolute authority over our hearts, over our minds, and in our lives.

This is true concerning the gifts of the Spirit also. First of all, we must remember the purpose for which the gifts are given, which is the proclamation of the gospel and the edification of the church; second, we must always acknowledge His Lordship over each gift given by the Spirit. He has absolute authority over each gift which He has given. We are servants of the Most High God, and He is our Lord; but one would think, by the way that some Christians act, that they were lord and He the servant. I do not say this disrespectfully, and I do not mean to be sacrilegious when I say it; but it is true. I have witnessed so much spiritual bigotry in some religious organizations; I have seen so much spiritual pride in the lives of some Christians, that it would appear that THEY held the lordship - that THEY were ruler - that THEY were the controller, and the Lord Jesus Christ was the servant.

I think of that sometimes when I hear some men and women pray, when they are so demanding of God. I fear and I tremble. My friend, we are but frail creatures of the dust, dependent upon God for every breath, dependent upon Him for the next beat of our heart. How dare we command Him to do anything! How dare any human being demand God to do something! He is God Almighty, and we must never forget it.

CHAPTER 7

Gift of Wisdom

Let us study some of the individual gifts of the Spirit, beginning with the one that many consider to be the greatest of the spiritual gifts, the Word of Wisdom. God is perfect and absolute wisdom, and through this gift of the Spirit, He gives to an individual a part of Himself, a part of something that is absolute perfection.

Some have suggested that the gift of wisdom is a natural gift, sanctified to the service of God. Since all wisdom comes from God, they contend that the consecration of a natural gift becomes a spiritual manifestation. But this is not so.

If we allow that this is the true interpretation of the word of wisdom, then every Bible teacher could claim to have this first and greatest gift of the Holy Spirit. It would thus be exceedingly difficult to draw the line of demarcation between the Sunday school teacher giving his interpretation of the lesson, and some experienced Bible expositor giving a deep study on an important doctrinal truth.

There are others who, because they possess some natural wisdom, feel that they have this wonderful gift of wisdom, suggesting that the word of wisdom is the ability to speak wisely, to exercise tact, to say a word 'in season' or to assist those who need counsel or admonition.

If this were the right interpretation of the word of wisdom, then the gift is more in evidence than we have supposed. There are a great many people, many of God's precious children, who are able to give a helpful word to others. In fact, all of us, as Christians, should be able to help those who have problems and difficulties.

But, watch it! The word of wisdom is a divine, a supernatural revelation of the mind and the purpose of God communicated by the Holy Spirit. There is only one who is perfect wisdom, just one. That is Almighty God, and this includes every member of the Trinity: God the Father, Jesus Christ the Son, and the Person of the Holy Spirit. No man has perfect wisdom. Even Solomon could not claim that.

Read carefully how the Bible states this gift: it is called the WORD of wisdom. It is God's wisdom imparted to man. It might be designated as the gift of the Word of God's Wisdom.

When God reveals His purpose to an individual, that person possesses a word of God's perfect wisdom. Quite apart from this supernatural gift of the Holy Spirit, the Lord is willing to guide believers in their daily affairs, to give them wisdom as required for any particular circumstance.

Every day of my life, I pray for divine wisdom. All of us need to pray for wisdom, His wisdom. But there is a gift that the Holy Spirit gives an individual where literally it is God's wisdom imparted to man, when God reveals His purpose to an individual. It is a supernatural gift from God and not a glorification of man's own natural wisdom or abilities.

CHAPTER 8

Gift of Faith

At the beginning of our study of the Gift of Faith, I shall answer a question that many have asked; Is the gift of faith necessary to work miracles? The answer is, No.

Some of you may be very surprised at my answer but remember something, each gift of the Spirit operates independently of the others. The Word of God found in Zechariah 4:6 is a very precious and vital part of my life: "Not by might nor by power, but by my Spirit, saith the Lord of hosts."

The portion preceding that verse tells us that the prophet saw the lampstand and the lamps of the Lampstand, each lamp operating independently of the other lamps; yet, they all received the oil from the main lampstand. It was the Holy Spirit who was the oil, and He was the One that was, literally, the power that kept each lamp burning. Each lamp was independent of the other, but the secret of power was found in the OIL of the Holy Spirit!

Likewise, each gift of the Spirit operates independently of the other gifts. So, when we come to the gift of faith, we see it operates independently and is not associated with the gift of Miracles, with divine healing or the healing of the physical body. One may have the gift of healing and not have the gift of faith; someone else may have the gift of Miracles and not have the gift of healing; and neither will they necessarily have the gift of faith. It is amazing how many of us have preconceived ideas and have put words into the mouth of God, words that are not there, and our thinking is contrary to the word of God.

See something here: "To one is given, by the Spirit, faith; to another the gift of healing; to another the working of miracles." These are separate gifts entirely. There are many who associate faith with the healing of the physical. The moment we talk about a man of great faith, they invariably associate him with miracles and with healing of the physical body. However, someone may have the gift of faith and that one may never have seen a miracle of healing! There are thousands, even tens of thousands of miracles, that have no bearing whatsoever on the healing of the physical. There can be great faith, one can have the gift of faith, and there will be no power in that life to pray for the healing of the sick.

Faith is not something that we carry around with us or something that we can put in our pockets and take out every once in a while, to look at and admire. I have often wished that I could put faith into a little capsule and pass it out! Then, whenever you had need of faith, I could send you the little capsule. But all I can tell you is that faith is not something that can be manufactured.

Let me give you an illustration. There are those who discount the fact that ravens fed Elijah twice a day with bread and flesh; who doubt that Daniel was divinely protected in the lion's den; and discredit entirely the reality of the three Hebrew children saved from the fiery furnace. Shadrach, Meshach and Abednego have suffered long at the hands of the liberalists; and so, have Jonah and the fish!

Now I am modern about everything except the Bible! I am as old-fashioned as the word of God, and I believe everything in this book. I am as old-fashioned as Daniel in the lion's den; as old-fashioned as Jonah and the whale. I believe that the Ravens literally fed Elijah - there isn't a doubt in my mind. There are miracles far greater than the healing of the physical body, as great as that is, and I am not underestimating the greatness of the healing of the physical. I believe that when God instructed Moses to pass his rod over the Sea, the gift of Miracles was needed to part the waters and a second gift of the Spirit, the gift of faith, was exercised for the passage to remain clear until all had passed over to dry land.

Daniel knew the thrill of the gift of faith in the lion's den. Shadrach, Meshach and Abednego knew the thrill of the gift of faith as they were cast into the fiery furnace. I do not believe there was one ounce of fear in the hearts or in the minds of these three Hebrew children when King Nebuchadnezzar commanded his mighty men to bind and cast them into the burning furnace. I believe that God gave Elijah the gift of faith when he prayed for the fire to consume the water and when he challenged the prophets of Baal. The gift of FAITH is one of the most glorious gifts of the Holy Spirit and in this gift of faith, the element of danger is often necessary for the gift to operate.

Those who have followed my ministry know of my deep respect and admiration for George Muller, a real saint of God. Whether or not he was conscious of the operation of the gift of faith in his life, I do not know; but I firmly believe God gave this man a gift of faith. He was head of one of the greatest orphans' homes the world has ever known. George Muller refused to beg for finances, did not approach men and women for support of this home; and yet those little children never missed a meal, they were never put to bed hungry. So far as anyone could tell - including those who knew him best- George Muller never worried, never lost a night's sleep worrying who would provide food or the necessary funds for the orphanage. He was given the gift of faith, and the gift of faith instills a peace and a calm in the time of need and danger.

Therefore, in brief, we can say that the gift of faith is a supernatural operation of the Holy Spirit in the experience of the possessor, which enables him to sustain an unwavering trust in God for his personal protection and provision. Faith is a gift that is given of God, a gift of the Holy Spirit.

CHAPTER 9

29

Gift of Miracles

God's gifts are a trust, placed in the hands or the body of an individual, and never forget that. No gift of the Spirit is ever given for personal glory or for "show." The Holy Spirit will magnify and glorify only one person, and that one person is Jesus Christ, the Son of the living God. Jesus Himself told us that the Holy Spirit "will glorify me" and He will glorify, He will magnify, He will bring attention to Jesus only. Therefore, we know that, when the Holy Spirit gives this wonderful trust to an individual, when He puts this trust into the hands or into the body of an individual, that one is out of order if he uses that gift to bring personal glory to himself, for any selfish gain, or for anything that is spectacular. That's the very reason that Paul, in writing to the Corinthian believers, began the 12th Chapter with the words, "I would not have you to be ignorant concerning the USE of these gifts." Each gift is to be held in subjection to the Lord, and His authority must be recognized in the use of all gifts.

As we begin a study of this Gift of Miracles, I caution you to be very careful that you do not confuse the gift of miracles with the gift of healing. It is amazing that so many folks have so trained their minds that whenever that word 'miracle' is used, invariably it is associated with divine healing. Yet, the gift of healing is one gift; faith is one gift; and the gift of miracles is another gift because the Word of God says, "to another the working of miracles." Therefore, the working of miracles is NOT the same as the gift of healing; neither is the gift of healing the same as the gift of faith.

What then is the working of miracles? What is the gift of Miracles? It's the supernatural demonstration of the power of God by which the laws of nature are either altered or controlled. God is still the mighty creator. He is still God Almighty. There is nothing impossible with Him. We forget that it is within His power to control the elements. We forget that it is still within His power to alter the laws of nature and even the laws of the universe. Why should one be so amazed at the miraculous? Why is it that human beings are so limited in their thinking that they refuse to accept anything that borders on the supernatural? God is the creator of all things, the one who formed the universe, created all flesh and breathed life into the nostrils of the first man Adam, and He has the power to alter His laws, the laws of nature. God is still at the controls, and the working of miracles is the supernatural demonstration of His power by which these laws are either controlled or altered.

Let us go a little farther. A miracle is a sovereign work of God, a manifestation of divine power, given to substantiate a message from God. In no instance does God perform a miracle or permit a miracle for the sake of the "spectacular" or to attract people to the miracle worker. The purpose behind God's miracles is to substantiate His message to the people.

It is apparent that there was greater evidence of miracles during the period of the Old Testament prophets than today. Why was this gift of Miracles more prevalent then? First of all, because we possess more spiritual light today. We have the Bible. We have the literal written word of God. Do you realize that the Old Testament saints didn't have the Bible as we have it, that those early Christians did not have the New Testament as a guide? Miracles in the Old Testament were more in evidence because the prophet established his divine authority before the people through the miracles he wrought. In a sense, therefore, miracles were his credentials.

In order to understand the ministry of God through miracles, we shall observe four different periods in scriptural history where the gift of miracles was recorded for our study and enlightenment. 1. Moses, as he led the children of Israel out of Egyptian bondage; 2. The miracles performed by Elijah and Elisha; 3. The ministry of Jesus; 4. The Day of Pentecost.

Miracles Through Moses

Let us turn to Exodus, Chapter 7, verse 9, and read where God commissioned Moses to lead the people of Israel out of Egyptian bondage: "When pharaoh shall speak unto you, saying, show a miracle for you: then thou shalt say unto Aaron, take thy rod and cast it before pharaoh, and it shall become a serpent." In other words, this miracle was used to establish Moses' divine authority before pharaoh. The 'rod/serpent' became his credential in order that pharaoh would know that Moses had been sent of God and was God's messenger. "Thou shalt talk thy rod, and cast it before pharaoh, and it shall become a serpent," That was a MIRACLE. God has a reason behind each Miracle He performs and allows. He never does anything promiscuously, and His miracles at the hand of Moses were wrought in connection with the deliverance of the children of Israel out of Egyptian bondage. Moses was given the power to work miracles for the benefit of Pharaoh, and as a sign to the children of Israel. Notice what God says in Exodus 7:3, "I will harden pharaoh's heart, and multiply my signs and my wonders in the land of Egypt." It was not what Moses was doing, but what GOD was doing through Moses. Continue to read on: "But pharaoh shall not hearken unto you, that I may lay my hand upon Egypt, and bring forth mine armies, and my people the children of Israel out of the land of Egypt by great judgements. And the Egyptians Shall know that I am the Lord, when I stretch forth mine hand upon Egypt, and bring out the children of Israel from among them." (Exodus 7:4,5).

How would pharaoh and the Egyptians know that God was working on behalf of the children of Israel? They knew by the signs and the miracles that came through the hand of Moses, who was given the power to work miracles. And how were the children of Israel to know that God had delivered them unto the leadership of Moses, that he was God's appointed ruler and leader? How could, they be sure? What evidence did they have? God, knowing human nature, knew that they, too, needed some outward sign, so the evidence came by the miracles at Moses' hand. The miracles confirmed Moses as God's appointed leader in Israel's deliverance from Egyptian bondage and that Moses was God's chosen instrument.

Miracles of Elijah and Elisha

In many instances throughout the Bible, we see more than one spiritual gift in operation simultaneously. The gifts of faith and Miracles, though entirely separate gifts of the Spirit, often go hand in hand and were manifested together as Moses led the children of Israel across the Red Sea. Again, these two gifts were wrought at the same time through Elijah who challenged the prophets of Baal on Mount Carmel. Turn to 1kings, Chapter 18, and read for yourself one of the greatest illustrations and evidences of God's gifts working through a human being.

A thousand times I have wished that I might have been there that day when Elijah called down the fire from heaven. There was action on that mountain, something was happening every minute! Elijah was not hallucinating. It was not a figment of his imagination when the fire of the Lord fell and consumed the sacrifice, consumed the stones of the alter and even the water in the trenches. It actually happened, but it did not happen because of one man's great faith. It was the gift of faith and the gift of Miracles given for the particular hour and need. God gave Elijah the faith to challenge the prophets of Baal, the faith to build the altar and prepare the sacrifice, to pour water over the altar until the trenches were overflowing- and then God gave the gift of Miracles!

And he put the wood in order, and cut the bullock in pieces, and laid him on the wood, and said, fill four barrels with water, and pour it on the burnt-sacrifice, and on the wood. And he said, do it the second time. And they did it the second time. And he said, do it the third time." (Had I been standing there near Elijah; I think I would have urged him to do it a fourth time!)

"And the water ran round about the altar; and he filled the trench also with water. And it came to pass at the time of the offering of the evening sacrifice, that Elijah the prophet came near, and said, Lord God of Abraham, Isaac, and of Israel, let it be known this day that thou art God in Israel, and that I am thy servant."(1 kings 18: 33-36).

God manifested His power through Elijah so that the people would know he was God's servant, that it was God Himself from whom he had received his authority, that all these things were done at His word, ordered of him, and that Elijah acted in the perfect will of God in all he did. This gift of Miracles was a trust that God had placed into the hands of a human being. It was not for Elijah's selfish gain or for show, but that God would be glorified and that all the people would know that God was God Almighty. (1 kings 18:39).

Through another prophet, Elisha, we see a glorious illustration of God's power to alter the laws of nature (11 kings 6:1-7). "And the sons of the prophets said unto Elisha, behold now, the place where we dwell with thee is too strait for us. Let us go, we pray thee, unto Jordan, and take thence every man a beam, and let us make us a place there, where we may dwell."

In other words, the young people felt much like some of today's youth, that their parents were too strait-laced, and they wanted to get away from home. "And he answered, Go ye. And one said, be content, I pray thee, and go with thy servants. And he answered, I will go. So, he went with them. And when they came to Jordan, they cut down wood."

Can't you just imagine these young people cutting down trees in the forest, many of them never having worked with their hands before? "But as one was felling a beam, the axe head fell into the water: and he cried, and said, Alas, master! For it was borrowed."

This young man was in trouble and he panicked. What was he going to do? The axe head was not his. It had slipped off the handle and had fallen into the Jordan River. What could he do to get it back? "And the man of God said, where fell it? And he showed him the place. And he cut down a stick, and cast it in thither; and the iron did swim. Therefore, said he, take it up to thee. And he put out his hand, and took it."

Here in the word of God we see that God altered the law of gravity for a brief moment through the gift of Miracles, and iron was made to literally "swim."

Miracles of Jesus

As we turn now to study the miracles in the New Testament, consider something that may be as new to you as it was to me when the Holy Spirit revealed His truth to my heart. Is there any difference between the gifts as exercised by the Lord Jesus Christ and the gifts that were demonstrated through the apostles of the early church? Is there a difference between the gifts manifested by Jesus and the gifts that He promised to every redeemed member of His body, to those who are a part of His church living today?

Immediately, there are those who will answer, 'yes.' They are dead sure that there is a difference between the gifts exercised by our Lord and the gifts manifested by the disciples. Some may even rebel against this question, but I urge you to listen carefully to what I say here. Did Jesus manifest His deity when He wrought His miracles or were they a result of the holy endowment of the Holy Spirit which He received at the River Jordan when the Spirit descended from heaven and rested upon Him in the form of a dove?

I know I have said it over and over again, but it is true; Jesus was as much God, as much deity and divinity, as though He were not man; and yet, He was as much man as though there was no deity whatsoever connected with Him. The Lord Jesus Christ, when He was upon the earth, ministered only as any other person so endowed with the power of the Holy Spirit. He voluntarily emptied Himself of any attributes that gave Him any direct connection with deity. This was absolutely necessary in order that He could be as much man as He was God. That is the reason why there were no miracles in those early years of His life. Miracles did not begin to happen until AFTER that glorious experience at the River Jordan. Then it was, for the first time in Jesus' earthly ministry, that the three persons of the Trinity were present at once. God Himself spoke in an audible voice and said: "This is My beloved Son, in whom I am well pleased."(Mathew 3:17)

In other words, God was saying, this is My Son, the Son of the Living God, but He has taken upon Himself the form of a man. In that instant, the Holy Spirit descended upon Jesus. The Holy Spirit took complete possession of Him and things began happening through His life. Miracles took place where there had been no miracles before and where no great manifestation of the deity of God, or the supernatural, had been witnessed. No, only AFTER the Holy Spirit came upon Jesus did these things occur, and we read of His first miracle at the wedding feast in Cana of Galilee (John 2:1-11).

Jesus was as truly the son of God BEFORE His baptism with the Holy Spirit as AFTER WARDS. If His miracles had been performed through a power that was His own as one of the Godhead, there would have been no necessity for the Holy Spirit to anoint Him with this supernatural power. Jesus laid aside His divine attributes, and for this period of His earthly life, He ministered only as a man anointed by the Spirit of God.

Miracles of the Day of Pentecost

Turn to the Gospel of John, Chapter 14, verse 12, and read Jesus' words: "He that believeth on me, the works that I do shall he do also," This scripture is not readily understood because it is very often taken out of context; and yet it offers one of our greatest inheritances as God's children. Why could Jesus say these words? Because He was so well aware that it was the power of the Holy Spirit in Him, working through Him, that enabled Him to perform miracles; and the same power was promised to His disciples, to you and to me!

There isn't one of us who hasn't thrilled to the miracles performed by the disciples of the early church. We know that "God wrought special Miracles by the hand of Paul" (Acts19: 11); Philip was caught away by the Spirit of the Lord as he came up out of the water following the baptism of the eunuch (Acts 8:39); and don't you wish you could have been there when peter, in prison, asleep between two soldiers, bound with two chains, awoke to see an angel who set him free from his bonds and guided him safely past the guards into the street? (Acts 12:5-11).

But we are still living in the Day of Pentecost! Jesus promised that "he that believeth on me, the works I do shall he do also." All that God asks of you, all that He asks of me, is that we yield our bodies as a temple of the Holy Spirit, that we yield ourselves as empty vessels. One of the reasons why He has to choose the base things, the most unlikely people in giving spiritual gifts to His children, is that no flesh shall glory in His presence, because no flesh has the power to do these supernatural things that the Holy Spirit does.

If there is any sadness in heaven, I believe it shall be when we actually see what might have been ours, what could have been ours, what He was wanting to do with us, in us and through us; but we were too stupid, or we lacked the vision so that we blocked Him here, or limited Him over there. Yet, the whole time we had the promise from the Master Himself: "He that believeth on me, the works that I do shall he do also." Why? Because of the person of the Holy Spirit. There are things in the miraculous realm that cannot be explained by human reasoning, but we can believe them as we acknowledge God and the fact that He works in a supernatural way. Wherever we find the Holy Spirit in evidence, we find the supernatural, the manifestation of God's power.

What, then, is the working of miracles? It is the supernatural demonstration of the power of God by which the laws of nature are controlled or altered. You and I can believe God for Miracles today in our own lives, and He will work through us as we accept the fact that God is still on His Throne for, we are heirs with Christ Jesus our Lord, and the only limit to His power lies within each of us. His gifts, the gifts of the Holy Spirit, are for His church, members of the Body of Christ, gifts for you and for me.

CHAPTER 10

Tongues

One morning when picking up my personal mail, l was handed a very imposing looking envelope. In the upper left-hand corner was printed, "United States Senate." Upon opening it, I found it had been written by a Senator's wife. She had been listening to our radio broadcasts and asked a question, a most important question, which may be one you have asked too. Let me quote just a few paragraphs from her letter:

"I missed your exposition on radio concerning the 'tongues movement.' I should so like to know your belief on this subject. These people seem to feel that they have something which the rest of us who are Christians lack. If it is of the Lord, why should I feel so embarrassed, so disgusted when I hear someone speaking in tongues?

"In the hospital recently, a group of these people visited me, and it was most embarrassing. One woman whom I know looks down her nose at me because I do not speak in tongues as she does. She teaches a Sunday School Class, is very active in religious circles, prayer groups, etc.; but she believes that she can live exactly as she pleases, do whatever she pleases because her belief in Christ and her speaking in tongues sets her apart from God's 'thou shalt not' laws.

"I do not mean to condemn someone for something that I do not understand or have not experienced, but please help me by answering my question. I missed your views on this subject because of maddening static and interference by adjacent stations."

First of all, let me say that I sincerely believe that the lack of teaching on this subject is one reason why so much reproach has been brought upon this beautiful spiritual experience. Therefore, I shall deal with the subject as simply as I know how; for good sound doctrinal teaching regarding this experience of being filled with the Spirit, and the speaking in tongues, is vitally needed in this hour. We will examine what the Word of God has to say, for no person can take issue with God's word. It is the highest authority in heaven and earth, and regardless of what has been taught by man, regardless of any theology, if it is contrary to God's word, there can be no dispute: GOD'S WORD IS ALWAYS RIGHT! All that I ask of you, as we study this subject, is that you allow your mind to be open to the Word of God. In answering the Senator's wife, I will begin with something that may seem very remote at first, and someone is sure to ask, "What connection is there between 1 Corinthians, Chapter 13, and Acts 2:4?" My answer to you is, EVERYTHING! We are dealing with the same person, the Holy Spirit - and remember that the Holy Spirit is a PERSON. Whenever the Holy Spirit is mentioned, some people immediately think of one thing: 'tongues', speaking in tongues! They have never become acquainted with the power of the Trinity or the ministry of the gifts that He gives. I want you to see the ministry of His gifts, I want you to see the fruits of the Spirit; and as truly as He gives gifts, there will be certain fruits from His gifts, fruits of the Spirit, evidences by which we know that which one possesses is real and genuine. Mathew 7:20, states: "By their fruits ye shall know them."

Whatever experience we receive from the Lord, that experience is personal and wholly private between the Master and the individual. The actual transaction cannot be seen by anyone, however near that person maybe, but the spiritual encounter will be substantiated by that one's actions and the life that He lives, by outward evidences of that which has taken place internally. Concerning one's salvation, the outward manifestations will allow no doubt as to whatever or not that person has been born again; and in exactly the same way, the fruits of the Spirit will be manifested in the life of the one who has been filled with the Spirit. That wonderful experience, when literally the Holy Spirit comes into a body and makes it the temple of the Holy Spirit, is something most sacred. His presence produces outward evidences which cannot be disguised, and these external affirmations are the fruits of the Spirit.

"Other Tongues"

Before we look into the various fruits of the Holy Spirit, let us examine the difference between the experience that the one hundred and twenty had in the Upper Room on the first day of Pentecost when "they began to speak with other tongues," and the GIFT of tongues.

"When the day of Pentecost was fully come, they were all with one accord in one place. And suddenly there came a sound from heaven as of a rushing mighty wind, and it filled all the house where they were sitting. And there appeared unto them cloven tongues like as of fire, and it sat upon each of them. And they were all filled with the Holy Ghost, and began to speak with other tongues." (Acts 2:1-4)

Jesus had promised that the Holy Ghost would come. He had told His disciples to tarry and wait for the Holy Ghost. And He came even as Jesus said He would come. They waited, Jesus kept His word, the Holy Spirit came, and they began to speak with other tongues "as the Spirit gave them utterance."

The Holy Spirit did it, and I'm all for it when the Holy Spirit does the work. Anything that He does, I can say 'Amen' to it, and I will accept it; but I must be dead sure that He is the one who is doing it. And this was the Spirit, for "they began to speak with other tongues as the Spirit gave them utterance." And there were dwelling at Jerusalem Jews, devout men, out of every nation under heaven. Now when this was noised abroad, the multitude came together, and were confounded, because that every man heard them speak in his own language." (Acts 2:4-6).

This wasn't just spiritual communication, it was literally that they communicated, every man in his own language. "And they were all amazed and marveled, saying one to another, Behold, are not all these which speak Galileans? And how hear we every man in our own tongue, wherein we were born?" (Acts 2: 7,8) By the Spirit of God, they were given the power of utterance in languages unknown to those who spoke! Every man heard one speak in his own language.

Therefore, 'speaking with other tongues' is the ability to preach the gospel in a language that one has never learned, enabling the preacher, the child of God, in the power of the Spirit, to stand up and witness, to teach and talk in the hearer's language without having studied to learn the language. I cannot tell you HOW the Holy Spirit does it, but I know it is scriptural.

Fruits of the Spirit

My friend, there is more to being filled with the Spirit than speaking in other tongues, MUCH more, and Paul begins the 13th Chapter of 1 Corinthians by saying: "Though I speak with the tongues of men and of angels, and have not love, I am become as sounding brass, or a tinkling cymbal." We have all known folk who 'sound off' but possess no power in their Christian life - no fruit, just noise - so let us analyze some of the fruits of the Spirit evidenced in the believer's lives, as named by Paul in his "love chapter."

" Love suffereth long..." There goes impatience. You say that you have been filled with the Spirit, that your body is a vessel of the Holy Spirit, but what about that impatience in your life? "Love is kind..." There is no room for unkindness. "Love envieth not..." There goes jealousy and where you find jealousy in a life and heart, you do not find the constant abiding presence of the Holy Spirit. Sometimes I feel that one of the most prevalent sins among Christians is the sin of jealousy, and yet the scripture teaches that "love envieth not." "Love vaunteth not itself..." There is no boasting. "Love is not puffed up..." There goes pride. If you have really been filled with Spirit, you will not look down your nose upon another with a spirit of bigotry, with Spiritual pride, and a better than thou attitude as if to say, "I have more Spirituality than you possess." I do not believe that one can truly be filled with the Holy Spirit and that vessel be a sacred sanctuary, while at the same time, spiritual bigotry is present in that life.

The greatest of all Christian graces is humility, and yet the writer of the letter from which I quoted tells of one who claims to be filled with the Spirit and is puffed up with Spiritual pride! That one who professes to be filled with the Spirit because of this experience, feels that God will be a little more lenient with her; that she has a special place with Him giving her a license, so to speak, to do anything she wants to do, to live any way she desires. Here again we are reminded of the old proverbs: "the things you do speak so loud, that I can't hear the things that you say."

If you don't live the life, don't profess it. By your actions, you are a stumbling block to others. The greatest compliment that can be paid a Christian is for an unbeliever to say, "I don't understand it, I am not spiritual myself, but I have confidence in what you believe because you live it." Again, I say, if you don't live it, don't profess it. You are only hurting the work of the Lord Jesus Christ.

Many times, the only Christ that the unsaved person sees today in the world is the Christian. YOU may be the only living Christ that your fellow employees or your neighbors see. The only Bible that the unsaved man or woman may read is the life of the person who professes to be born again. That is what the scripture means: "For me to live... For you to be living... for us to be alive today, is Christ." We represent Him, and He is love; and we must manifest His love through our lives; and it's the Holy Spirit who gives us that power, that enables us to be a witness, to represent Him, to manifest His love. This is what it means to be filled with the Holy Spirit. We need to realize what it actually means to be a Christian. Great is our responsibility.

"Love doth not behave itself unseemly, seeketh not her own, is not easily provoked, thinketh no evil; rejoiceth not in iniquity, but rejoiceth in the truth..." There goes selfishness, fault-finding, backbiting and malice. "Love beareth all things..." There is no more complaining. "Love believeth all things..." Mistrust goes. "Love hopeth all things, endureth all things..." Anxiety, worry and despondency go.

When it comes down to the final analysis, all the fruits of the Spirit can be summed up in a single word - LOVE. "For me to live is Christ" (Philippians 1:21), and Christ is love. That is the real evidence that one has the Holy Spirit dwelling within, manifesting Himself through that life. You can literally 'love' a neighbor into the kingdom of God, you can win a member of your family to Christ through love. Wherever you find the abiding presence of the Holy Spirit, you will find LOVE. LOVE conquers all things.

Gift of Tongues and Interpretation of Tongues

Now we come to the gift of Tongues, which is the power of utterance in languages unknown to the speaker, a gift given to certain individuals in the church by the Spirit of God. This gift is capable of interpretation by means of an equally supernatural gift, in order that these utterances may thereby become intelligible to the assembly. They are given for the edification of the church (the body of saints) and for the glory of God.

When the gift of interpretation is in operation together with the gift of tongues, the two are equivalent to prophecy. The gift of interpretation can be compared to the interpretation of a foreign tongue into our native language by one who knows both languages. It is a supernatural endowment of the Spirit, and implies no natural knowledge by the interpreter of the language spoken in tongues.

This, the interpretation, is not received by close attention to the words of the one speaking in tongues. Interpretation is received by close concentration in spirit upon the Lord, who alone gives the interpretation. The words are therefore given by revelation; and if it is the Spirit of the Lord doing the speaking and the Spirit doing the interpreting, no message will ever be contrary to the word of God. He will neither add to nor take away from the Bible, but all will be in perfect harmony; and the one who has been given the gift of tongues, or the gift of interpretation, will never use the gift to draw attention to himself. The gifts will be used for the glory of God.

Please let me bare my soul to you, and I pray the Lord will give me the words to express myself so that you will understand. There are many who are boasting of having some gift of the Spirit, bringing reproach on something most sacred and holy. It is my firm conviction and my own personal experience that if the Holy Spirit has given an individual a gift, that gift and that trust will be so sacred to that one that he will not exploit it nor boast about it, or even talk of it. I have had spiritual experiences that are so sacred to me that I have never spoken of them to any human being. One does not boast of these things, and any saint of God to whom a gift has been given will not capitalize on it.

Over and over again I have met those who will say, "Oh, Miss Kuhlman, I have the gift of tongues..." Now, you know me well enough to realize that I believe in speaking in tongues. I have to believe it because it's in the Bible. But when one has been given this sacred gift, he will not talk about it, capitalize on it, exploit it or use it to draw attention to himself. Too many people are using tongues for their own selfish gain or for recognition.

I'll just pause a moment here until you get your equilibrium back again! But somebody needs to speak out on this matter. We need to come back to the word of God. Some of you have gone so far that it has been many a day since you have taken the scriptures and have stood purely on "thus saith the Lord." There are too many people ADDING TO the Bible.

You will admit, we readily condemn those who are taking from the Bible's truths. We condemn the man who stands in his pulpit and label him a "modernist" when he doesn't preach the atonement, when he does not teach divine healing or the deity and divinity of Jesus Christ. It is easy for us to denounce the one who is taking from the word of God. And it's true that there are those who are guilty of this sin of omission. But there are also literally hundreds today who are adding to the word of God. They are putting words into the mouth of Jesus that He never uttered. They are putting things in the scriptures that are unscriptural.

We have every right to see the gifts and the fruits of the Spirit in operation in our churches today. No Bible student, no theologian, can prove to me from the word of God that the power of God was "turned off" when Jesus went back to the father to take the position of great High Priest. Everything that happened in the early church, everything that took place in Paul's ministry, the same power manifested by peter and the other disciples after the Day of Pentecost, should be in operation and manifested in the church today because we are still living in that dispensation, the Day of Pentecost. But that does not mean that we are at liberty to use the gifts wherever and however we will. "The spirits of the prophets are subject to the prophets" (1 Corinthians 14:32), and if one is gifted of God, that one is to hold that gift in subjection to the Lord Jesus Christ and not make a spiritual nuisance of himself. Our blessed Lord's authority must be recognized in the use of all gifts, including the gift of tongues.

Let me go into this matter a little further. If, for instance, God has given you some particular gift of the Spirit, you are not to use that gift whenever you see fit; but only in subjection to the Lord Jesus Christ. All gifts must be used in subjection to the Lord Himself.

Remember something - and never forget it. The Holy Spirit is given to the believer for one purpose and one purpose only: for SERVICE! Some have not realized the purpose of this wonderful experience of being filled with the Spirit, and as a result have misappropriated the power of the Spirit. The Holy Spirit is for service and not for our own personal benefit and enjoyment. We, as

Christians, filled with the Holy Spirit, share the responsibility of winning the lost to Christ. Jesus said, "ye shall receive power, after that the Holy Ghost is come upon you." (Acts 1:8). Power for what? To witness for Him! You don't have to ask someone," Have I been filled with the Spirit?" Instead, ask yourself the question, "How many souls have I won to the Lord Jesus Christ since my experience?"

There are those who ask, "Is the speaking in tongues the evidence of having been filled with the Spirit?" My friend, there are those who have spoken in tongues when they were filled with the Spirit; but I contend that the SCRIPTURAL evidence comes from the lips of Jesus Himself, the highest authority in heaven and earth, an evidence that cannot be counterfeit... "Ye shall receive POWER..."

Oh, that glorious, that marvelous, mighty power that will take charge of the mind, that power that will take human lips, fill a physical body with His anointing! There is no counterfeit for this power, it is something for which there is no substitute. It is the power to witness, the power to win souls, the power to lead men and women to the Lord Jesus Christ.

CHAPTER 11

11

Gift of Prophecy

It is most unfortunate that there are Christians who have allowed themselves to be 'sold short.' By this, I mean that they are missing so much by believing those who teach that the gifts of the Spirit ceased with the early church. Anything that peter received from God, anything that John was given, any gift that was manifested through the members of the early church is for Christians today. Don't let anybody 'sell you short' when it comes to the things of the Spirit.

"To another is given by the Spirit prophecy." What is this gift of prophecy? It is very simple, and it is clearly explained in 1 Corinthians 14:3: "He that prophesieth speaketh unto men to edification, and exhortation, and comfort." Revelation is not mentioned. Prophecy in the New Testament sense is not FORETELLING, but TELLING FORTH the word of God and the Gospel of Jesus Christ.

Sometimes I think we get very confused when it comes to this gift of prophecy. There are those who have hallucinations that they have been given some gift to prophesy beyond that which is in the word of God, and that is where fanaticism enters.

Beloved, the Holy Spirit will never give to an individual, He will not give to any man or any woman, more than that which is written in the word of God. Therefore, if someone should say that they have the gift of prophecy and will give something contrary to the word of God, or add to the word of God, that one is committing a gross sin, and the Holy Spirit has no part whatsoever in what is prophesied.

False doctrines and false cults are born from such teachings, and we are cautioned in Revelation 22:18 lest we be misled: "if any man shall add unto these things, God shall add unto him the plagues that are written in this book."

There can be no doubt as to what is meant by the gift of prophecy, and the simplest way I know to explain this gift is to say that it is a gift of communication. Oh, to be the vessel used of the Holy Spirit as He speaks through lips of clay, taking control of the mind, communicating to others the true meaning of the word of God! Along with the gift of the word of knowledge and the word of wisdom, I personally covet that gift of prophecy where I may stand before men and women, under the anointing of the Holy Spirit, and communicate through Him the word of the Living God that it would become life to that one who hears my voice, bringing spiritual understanding and acceptance of Christ as Saviour and Lord; that through understanding of the word that one seeks to be filled with the Holy Spirit, that the Bible becomes alive, and its truths revealed. Jesus had that marvelous gift of the Holy Spirit.

No one ever sat in His presence without fully understanding everything He said. What He spoke was said so simply that children could comprehend; yet, in the natural, God's word is so profound that the most intellectual person cannot fathom it, reading it but having no understanding. The Bible is different from any other book in the world. Only the Holy Spirit can reveal God's word: "Flesh and blood hath not revealed it unto thee, but my father which is in heaven." (Matthew 16:17). Through the gift of prophecy, the Holy Spirit gives to an individual the power to communicate; and as a result, the listener receives an understanding of the word of God and grows spiritually, going deep into the things of the Lord.

It is wonderful to see sick bodies healed by the power of God, but there is something far greater than a physical Miracle.

The greatest thrill I can know is for someone to say: "As I listened to you bring your message from the word of God, I had an understanding of the Bible, an insight into the love and tender mercy of God the Father, seeing the character of Jesus Christ as I never knew or understood before." That is the gift that comes only from the Holy Spirit, the Gift of prophecy.

CHAPTER 12

Gift of Discerning of Spirits

"...to another discerning of Spirits." 1 Corinthians 12:10) Let me begin our study of this gift by saying that some seem to think there is a contradiction in God's word, a conflict between the Gift of Discerning of Spirits and the 'trying of Spirits' mentioned in 1 John 4:1. These are not one and the same; there is a distinct difference between the two.

When John said to "try the spirits," he was not talking about the same thing that Paul wrote about in 1 Corinthians 12:10, the discerning of Spirits. Believers are instructed to 'try' or 'test' the spirits to find out if it is the spirit of God, the spirit of Christ, the Holy Spirit; or whether it is the spirit of the evil one, or demon power, and the wrong spirit.

How are we to test the Spirits? We test the Spirits by the written, revealed, inspired word of God. Any spirit that operates contrary to the word of God is not of God. This is one of the reasons why it is vitally important to know what the Bible says. Many have gotten away from the Bible, so far away from the teaching of Christ, that they scarcely recognize the scriptures when they hear them taught. Get back to the Bible! Regardless of denomination or where you have your church membership, humanity needs to come back again to "thus saith the Lord," and the word of God. In talking about 'trying the Spirits,' John cautioned believers to put the spirits to the test, and to test them by the written, revealed, inspired word of God.

On the other hand, this gift that the Holy Spirit gives, this wonderful gift of Discerning of Spirits that is mentioned in the 12th Chapter of 1 Corinthians, is something entirely different from 'trying the Spirits.' Like any other spiritual gift, the gift of Discerning of Spirits is not a natural judgement. Some people are born with a natural sensibility: they are sensitive, responsive, and receptive to certain things with a natural intuitiveness. But that which is spoken of in the word of God here, the gift of discerning of Spirits, is not the natural judgement that some people possess. It is not merely having the supposed ability to detect demon power in people, which any born-again, Spirit-filled person should be able to perceive, especially when one is sensitive to the spirit. No, that is not what is involved in the discerning of Spirits.

Looking back, I recall those who were dead sure that they had the gift of discernment, when all on earth they possessed was the spirit of judging. They judged their neighbors, and they judged everybody in their church. You have them in your church, too, in your own assembly, those who can tell you what is wrong with everyone. Forget it! This is not of the Holy Spirit.

What is this gift of discerning of Spirits? How should one define this gift? The Discerning of Spirits is the gift of the Holy Spirit by which the possessor is enabled to see into the spirit world.

Angels are real to me, and when David said, "he shall give his angels charge over you," he meant exactly that. This very hour, I believe that there are legions of angels who are protecting God's people, positioned on the battle front against the forces of evil. I feel sorry for the one who does not have a godly parent or some saint who is praying for him. The greatest power that God has given to any individual is the power of prayer.

He has literally tens of thousands of angels who guard, who protect, who care for the children of God. Little do I know, little do you know how near danger came; and had it not been for the protection of the angel of the Lord, we would have suffered harm. That's scriptural. Yet, I cannot tell you that I have really seen an angel.

When an angel appears in spirit form in the presence of a number of God's people, only those who have the gift of the discerning spirits will see the angel. Ezekiel saw the overwhelming revelation of the glory of the Lord, with the cherubim beneath the throne. No one else saw it. Later, while Ezekiel was sitting in his house with the elders of Israel before him, he was carried away in the spirit to Jerusalem, and he saw the things that were taking place in that city. The Holy Spirit had given him a gift whereby he could see the things that were taking place in that city. Read it in Ezekiel, Chapter 37.

The stoning of Stephen is another great example of that which I am trying to explain, and it is best that I let the word of God speak for itself. Turn to

Acts 7:54-58: "When they heard these things, they were cut to the heart, and they gnashed on him with their teeth. But he, being full of the Holy Ghost..." (Remember something, this is BEFORE Stephen's martyrdom. He was standing in the council, not on the street where he was stoned. He was not dying at this moment, as some would have you think. He was not in a comma. He had all of his senses). Stephen, being full of the Holy Ghost, "looked up steadfastly into heaven, and saw the glory of God, and Jesus standing on the right hand of God, and said Behold, I see the heavens opened, and the son of man standing on the right hand of God. Then they cried out with a loud voice, and stopped their ears, and ran upon him with one accord, and cast him out of the city, and stoned him."

God gave Stephen that glorious gift of revelation, of looking into the spirit world, before he was driven into the street and out of the city, before a stone ever touched his body. I do not believe that there was one in that council, not an elder or a scribe, who saw what Stephen saw. Even that man nearest him never saw what he saw.

Let me ask the question and answer it again: How should one define the gift of the discerning of the spirits? The discerning of Spirits is a gift of the Holy Spirit given to an individual, whereby the possessor of that gift is enabled to see into the spirit world.

CHAPTER 13

See Jesus!

In summarizing our study of the Gifts of the Spirit, let us turn to the Second Chapter of 1 Corinthians, starting with verse One. Here Paul is writing to those who have had that wonderful experience of having been born again. He is writing to those who knew all about being filled with the Spirit. They were not ignorant regarding the power of the Holy Ghost.

"And I, brethren, when I came to you, came not with excellency of speech or of wisdom, declaring unto you the testimony of God. For I determined not to know anything among you, save Jesus Christ, and him crucified. And I was with you in weakness, and in fear, and in much trembling. And my speech and my preaching was not with enticing words of man's wisdom, but in demonstration of the Spirit and of power: that your faith should not stand in the wisdom of men, but in the power of God. Howbeit we speak wisdom among them that are perfect: yet not the wisdom of this world, nor of the princes of this world, that come to nought: But we speak the wisdom of God in a mystery, even the hidden wisdom, which God ordained before the world unto our glory: which none of the princes of this world knew: for had they known it, they would not have crucified the Lord of glory." 1 Corinthians 2:1-8.

Sometimes, I think that we get so involved with doctrine that we lose sight of the Lord Jesus Christ entirely. When I hear Christian leaders in conversation, when I associate with those who are well acquainted with the deeper things of the Spirit, I fear that some are getting involved with controversial doctrines, losing sight of the person of Jesus Christ. I have stood on the sidelines listening to Christian discuss spiritual things, I have heard Christian leaders debate doctrine such as eternal security. They differ as to the mode of baptism, whether to speak in tongues or not to speak in tongues. They disagree as to the initial evidence of having been filled with the Spirit.

Whether it is baptism, being filled with the Spirit, tongues, or any of the gifts of the Spirit, they are ALL secondary to Jesus Christ the Son of God, and all of these things that we call doctrine must compliment Jesus. Remember, the whole Bible, from Genesis through Revelation, is the revelation of one person, Jesus

Christ. The Holy Spirit is very careful under all circumstances to magnify Jesus, and before Jesus went away, He made it very clear that the Holy Spirit would come after His ascension and take up residence upon this earth. Jesus said, "He (the Holy Spirit) shall glorify me." (John 16:14) That's the work of the Holy Spirit!

I believe in the doctrines of the church that the scriptures teach. I believe in water baptism, I believe in immersion, I believe in the power of God, I believe in being filled with the Spirit, I believe in the gifts of the Spirit. But what I am trying to say is that we are using some of these things that are secondary to overshadow the one of the greatest importance, the person of Jesus Christ the Son of God. The Bible is not the revelation of the Holy Spirit. The Bible from beginning to end is the revelation of Jesus Christ.

I challenge you to show me from the holy scriptures anything that is more important than Jesus, for It is what we do with Jesus that marks the destiny of the never-dying soul of a human being. Jesus, the person of God's son, Deity and Divinity, is the message of the church; and the church is the pillar and the foundation of this truth, the institute in the world in which this truth, is deposited. The church as a whole, and Christian as individuals, must make known to a lost and dying world the way of salvation through the Son of the Living God. There is nothing more important than Jesus.

CHAPTER 14

Our Great High Priest

The Apostle Paul knew the source of his power: "I determined not to know anything among you, save Jesus Christ, and him crucified." (1 Corinthians 2:2). He did not try to analyze God nor the power of God. He preached Jesus and Jesus only.

Aside from whatever ability he possessed and all his acquired learning, Paul knew there would be no conversions, no transformation of lives, the power of sin could not be broken in the lives of men and women, without the manifestation of God's power. Nothing would happen unless there be the convicting and transforming power of the Holy Spirit. How did Paul know? Because Jesus said so Himself: "Nevertheless I tell you the truth; It is expedient for you that I go away; for if I go not away, the comforter (the Holy Ghost) will not come unto you; but if I depart, I will send him unto you."(John 16:7).

And this is what happened! We know that Jesus arrived in heaven, that He 'made it' to the right hand of God the Father and is now in position of great High Priest. How can we be sure the connection was made as He promised? Because God's plans followed on schedule. The Holy Spirit came on the Day of Pentecost even as Jesus said He would come to begin His work: "he will reprove the world of sin"(His convicting power); "and of righteousness, and of judgement: of sin, because they believe not on me; of righteousness, because I go to my father, and ye see me no more; of judgement, because the prince of this world is judged. I have yet many things to say unto you, but ye cannot bear them now. Howbeit when he, the Spirit of truth, is come, he will guide you into all truth: for he shall not speak of Himself..." In other words, Jesus said that the Holy Spirit will not glorify Himself; He will not promote Himself, "but whatsoever he shall hear, that shall he speak: and he will show you things to come. HE SHALL GLORIFY ME..."(John 16:8-14)

Sometimes in our ignorance, we are glorifying everything under God's heaven except Jesus. Regardless of your experiences in the Spirit, if, in your life, you are glorifying another person or a personality other than Jesus Christ the Son of

God, it is not the Holy Spirit who is doing the glorifying. Why do I say this? Because Jesus Himself said "the Holy Spirit will glorify me."

The Holy Spirit will never draw attention to another personality; He will never draw attention to any man or woman. The more spiritual a person becomes, the more he will draw attention from himself and lift up Jesus. At no time did the Holy Spirit draw attention to Paul. In speaking of himself, Paul considered himself the least of the least, the chiefest of sinners; but we are seeing some Christians today whose egos are puffed up by their own Spirituality. Remember the words of Jesus, and there is no greater authority: "He shall glorify me: for he shall receive of mine, and shall show it unto you. All things that the father hath are mine: therefore, said I, that he shall take of mine, and shall show it unto you."(John 16:14,15).

Let me repeat again something that I said earlier: everything that the Holy Spirit does compliments Jesus. If you have received a gift of the Spirit, that gift that He has entrusted to you will compliment and magnify Jesus if it's of the Spirit. It will be used under His leadership and under His control. If that gift is manifested in an assembly or in the church, it will be used only as it glorifies and magnifies Jesus. Gifts of the Spirit are capacities for service, and that service is to lead men and women into the saving knowledge of the Christ, the Son of God.

CHAPTER 15

The Mysteries of God

"And I was with you in weakness, and in fear, and in much trembling. And my speech and my preaching was not with enticing words of man's wisdom, but in demonstration of the Spirit and of power... not the wisdom of this world... but we speak the wisdom of God in a mystery." (1 Corinthians 2:3-7)

Paul, under the anointing of the Holy Spirit, wrote these words to the church at Corinth. He was eloquent, learned and masterful; yet, he was fearful, and he was awed by the greatness of the Mysteries of God.

What were Paul's fears? He was not speaking of physical weaknesses. He had no mental weakness. He was not fearful of bodily harm, of personal enemies, or the criticism of men. He had no fear for his position. It was not a natural fear concerning himself.

Then why did Paul write these words? There was fear, there was alarm lest... and may I borrow a Biblical phrase here? ...lest the "trumpet should give uncertain sounds!" When it comes to spiritual things, there are no words in the human vocabulary to express what we want to say. So great was Paul's sense of weakness and fear, so profound was his lack of trust in himself to give forth the Mysteries of God that had been revealed to his heart, so overwhelming was the responsibility weighing upon Paul's spirit, that he quaked, and he trembled.

What are these Mysteries of God which Paul was talking about? The unregenerate man cannot comprehend that in a split second a man and his desires are changed. How can one pass from death unto life instantly and become a new creature in Christ Jesus? How can it be that the things he once loved he now hates, and the things he hated he now loves?

"How can one be born again?" was the question that Nicodemus asked Jesus. All humanity holds in common a physical birth; but there is another birth, a spiritual birth, which remains a mystery to our natural intellect. We are born anew as Christ is received, when our sins are forgiven, and we pass from death unto life.

Medical science declares it is impossible for a man whose physical body is saturated with alcohol as a result of living the life of a drunkard for years to stop drinking instantly. The shock to the physical is such that the human body will not be able to withstand the sudden change. Yet, literally, thousands of men and women can bear witness to the fact that instantly that desire left them when they accepted Christ as Saviour. That desire for alcohol was taken out by the very roots and that one's system was cleansed so thoroughly that it was as if he had never touched alcohol. For the first time in years, desires were normal.

My friends, I never stand before the open casket of someone who trusted me to give them the word of God, but that I stand and pray this simple prayer to my Heavenly father: "Father, I gave it to them the best that I knew how. If I have failed, forgive me." Only God knows the responsibility that there is in the giving forth of the word of Everlasting life to lost and dying men and women.

Yes, Paul stood head and shoulders above any other spiritual leader of his day for he knew the law well, and he was learned in all respects. But when it came to that which God had revealed and entrusted to him, when it concerned spiritual things and the Mysteries of God, he came with great trembling, he came with fear. Why? Because he knew that what he did was in the demonstration of the Spirit, it was supernatural power.

For just a moment, let me lift the lid of my heart and tell you about the person of Kathryn Kuhman when she walks off the stage from behind the pulpit after a great Miracle service, having seen the manifestation of God's power in the healing of sick bodies. You may think that I must feel so satisfied and so rewarded, and we'll repay. I'll tell you frankly, I walk off that stage with much fear and much trembling, thinking that there is so much more. I feel like a little child standing by the seashore picking up a pebble here, and a pebble there, admiring them, while the great sea rolls before me. We are only skimming the surface. There is so much MORE in Jesus Christ. There is so much MORE in the power of God than you, or I can realize, more than can be learned by study, or speculation. There's so much more in this mystery of God, revealed only through the HOLY SPIRIT. Not one has ever drained the resources of God or received all that He has in store for that life. There's more for me, there's more for you, and I challenge you to start today possessing your possessions.

CHAPTER 16

None of Self, All of Thee

"Oh, the bitter pain and sorrow that a time could ever be when I proudly said to Jesus, 'All of self and none of Thee."

"Yet He found me; I beheld Him Bleeding on the accursed tree; And my wistful heart said faintly some of self and some of Thee."

"Day by Day His tender mercy, Healing, helping, full and free, brought me lower, while I whispered - less of self, and more of Thee!" " Higher than the highest heavens, Deeper than the deepest sea, Lord, thy love at last has conquered: None of self and ALL of Thee!"

Theodore Monod penned these verses many years ago, expressing what is deeply within my own heart.

If you have not made that full surrender to Jesus, do it now. He will fill the emptied vessel with the Holy Spirit, you will know the demonstration of His power, and He will entrust to you His gifts, 'dividing to you severally as He will.' Then your life will glorify and compliment Jesus and you will find that His gifts are wholly the work of the Spirit, capacities for service in leading men and women into the saving knowledge of God's Son.

God bless you!

About Kathryn Kuhlman

Kathryn Kuhlman was born in 1907 in Concordia, Missouri, USA. In her early years as a young girl, she was known for her "independence, self-reliance and a desire to do things her way." These were characteristics that Kathryn would have to learn to take to the cross so that she should become totally dependent and reliant upon God. Her father was Baptist and her mother was Methodist and an excellent Bible teacher; So Kathryn received some of the finest Bible teachings at home.

Around 1924, Kathryn became acquainted with the healing ministry of Dr. Charles S. Price in Oregon where she also learned of the baptism of the Holy Spirit. In 1935, she established an evangelistic ministry in Denver Colorado auditorium that held 2000 people. She had no denominational affiliation. From 1938 to 1946, Kathryn went through a time of trial, heart-searching, and surrendering to the will of God. When she emerged out of her wilderness, she moved to Franklin, and from Franklin to Pittsburg, Pennsylvania, which became the base of post-World War-II ministry.

Kathryn had a burden for souls. Speaking to a group in Washington, D.C. She said, "I can only tell you that with my conversion, there came this terrific burden for souls. When you think of Kathryn Kuhlman, think only of someone who loves your soul, not someone who is trying to build something – only for the kingdom of God, that's all – souls, souls, souls! Remember! I gave my life for the sole vision of lost souls. And with my conversion, there came this terrific burden for lost souls."

Miracles

The first notable miracle occurred in her meeting in 1947, a woman had been healed of a tumor. A few days later, a war veteran who had been declared legally blind from an industrial accident had his eyesight restored. In her meetings, Kathryn placed less emphasis on faith and more emphasis on the Holy Spirit. She developed such a close relationship with the Holy Spirit, that one minister said: "It was like they were talking back and forth to each other, and you couldn't tell where Kathryn started and the Holy Spirit left off. It was a oneness."

Overseas Missions Stations

Kathryn Kuhlman said: "God didn't call me to build buildings, set up big offices, and have a huge staff." Kathryn did not feel called to build buildings for her ministry. Instead, the Kathryn Kuhlman Foundation occupied four small rooms in Pittsburg. Her facilities were unbelievably small in comparison to other Christian organizations that did not have the large outreach that the Kathryn Kuhlman Foundation had. Even her staff that manned the offices was considered to be a skeleton staff, but they were dedicated trusted people. Yet David Wilkerson said: "... the Kathryn Kuhlman Foundation had a worldwide pulpit."

Many mission stations had been erected overseas and each was presented debt-free to the native people as a gift from the Kathryn Kuhlman Foundation.

1. Corn Island, Nicaragua, Central America

2. Boaco, Nicaragua, Central America

3. Waspam, Nicaragua, Central America

4. Choluteca, Honduras, Central America

5. San Isidro, Costa Rica

6. Esteli, Nicaragua, Central America

7. Thakurpukur, India

8. Macau

9. Hong Kong Roof-Top School

10. Cotonou, Dahomey, West Africa

11. Mar del Plata, Argentina, South America

12. Santa Lucia, Nicaragua, Central America

13. Taipei, Formosa

14. Pretoria, South Africa

15. Johannesburg, South Africa

16. Rustenburg, South Africa

17. East London, South Africa

18. Kuala Lumpur, Malaysia

19. Surabaja, Indonesia

20. Viet Nam Chapel (Tin Lanh Military Chapel)

21. Ranger Clinic, Saigon, Viet Nam

22. Bible School Reconstruction, Managua, Nicaragua

23. Kathryn Kuhlman Memorial Church, Nairobi, East Africa

24. Kathryn Kuhlman Memorial Church, El Salvador, Central America

Equipment, hot lunches, education, and spiritual instruction were provided for Chinese children attending the Hon Kong roof-top school.

She also financially supported staff and a paraplegic ward in Saigon, Vietnam. After her homecoming, the last two were erected, with the Memorial Church in El Salvador paid for by gifts from her Canadian friends.

Kathryn Kuhlman Foundation donated hospital supplies and equipment to the Cong Hoa Military Hospital.

Time Magazine said: "She is, in fact, a veritable one-woman Shrine of Lourdes." Kathryn said: "I just carry a water bucket for the Lord." She said: "What I have is something that any Christian could have if he would pay the price of full surrender and yieldedness. I am absolutely dependent on the mercy of Lord Jesus Christ. I am dependent on the power of the Holy Spirit in exactly the same way that Jesus was when he was here in the flesh and walked this earth."

The Power of God Began to Fall

A diverse multitude of people came from afar to experience the awesome presence of God. They arrived at the Shrine Auditorium in chartered buses from Portland, Oregon, and Las Vegas. Delegations came from all over the world.

The power of God began to fall. Soon the aisles were crowded with those claiming they have been healed.

Kathryn was invited to minister in many cities. Las Vegas was one of those cities. The Las Vegas City Auditorium with its seating capacity of 8000 was filled and several thousand were left outside. Bus-loads of people came from Reno, Phoenix, Los Angeles, and elsewhere. Chartered planes flew people in from Hawaii, Auckland, St. Louis, Minneapolis, Seattle, and Denver.

"When I made a full and complete surrender of everything to Jesus, the Holy Spirit took the empty vessel, and that's all that He asks." "When I yielded to Him, body, soul and spirit, when I gave him everything, all there was of me, I knew then, beloved what the scripture means: 'If a man will follow me, let him take his cross.' " The cross is a symbol of dying to self.

Radio and Television

Kathryn continued to reach people where they were, whether it was through her miracle services, radio programs, or television. Hundreds of thousands of lives were touched by the power and presence of God through her ministry.

Fifty stations carried her thirty-minute broadcasts, five days a week, covering most of the nation; in Canada; and overseas broadcasts reaching much of Europe. For the last ten years of her life, her weekly half-hour television programs (produced at CBS in Los Angeles) were shown throughout the United States and Canada. Many of her radio sermons and television programs from the "I Believe in Miracles" series are available today.

Kathryn hungered for the deeper things of God and thereby was led by the Holy Spirit to learn the deeper truths of the cross.

Kathryn Kuhlman died on February 20, 1976, as a faithful "handmaiden of the Lord" and her legacy continues today.